THE TUTTLE TWINS
and their
SPECTACULAR
SHOW
BUSINESS

Books in The Tuttle Twins series:

The Tuttle Twins Learn About the Law
The Tuttle Twins and the Miraculous Pencil
The Tuttle Twins and the Creature from Jekyll Island
The Tuttle Twins and the Food Truck Fiasco
The Tuttle Twins and the Road to Surfdom
The Tuttle Twins and the Golden Rule
The Tuttle Twins and the Search for Atlas
The Tuttle Twins and their Spectacular Show Business
The Tuttle Twins and the Fate of the Future

Find them all at TuttleTwins.com

ISBN 978-1-943521-21-0

Boyack, Connor, author.
Stanfield, Elijah, illustrator.
The Tuttle Twins and their Spectacular Show Business/ Connor Boyack.

Cover design by Elijah Stanfield
Edited and typeset by Connor Boyack

Printed in the United States

10 9 8 7 6

To John Pestana

For demonstrating the impact
an entrepreneur can have.

"That is why... I am the one who did it!" the actor dramatically declared.

The Tuttle twins were mesmerized by the plot twist in the musical they were watching. It was their first experience watching a performance on Broadway and they were hooked!

"That was amazing!" Emily exclaimed as the Tuttle family exited the theater. "I wish we had stuff like this back home."

The family chatted about the play as they walked through Times Square. The twins enjoyed the sights and delicious foods of New York City, but the theater had become the highlight of their family vacation.

"I once dreamed of being on Broadway," Mrs. Tuttle said as she twirled in the air. "I loved doing theater when I was younger."

Mr. Tuttle booked a ride with his phone as the twins took one last look at the bright city lights. Soon their car arrived and they were off to the airport to catch their flight home.

"Let's watch Shark Pool!" Ethan suggested once the plane had taken off.

The Tuttle family loved watching the television show that featured *entrepreneurs*—people who identify a need and start a business that can help meet that need. The entrepreneurs each tried to convince the "sharks" to give them *capital*—money to start or grow their business.

In exchange, the sharks were offered *equity*—part of the ownership of the business.

SHARK POOL

One of the entrepreneurs was offering the sharks an opportunity to help a company he started to sell self-tying shoes for children and people with disabilities. He wanted $350,000 and was willing to give up 10% of his business to an interested shark.

The sharks thought the shoes were stylish and tied themselves really well. "And there's nothing else like these out there," one observed. "I'm interested."

"I love unique businesses that don't have much competition," another said. "I'll make you an offer."

In the end, the sharks teamed up to give the entrepreneur the capital he was seeking. "That's going to be a very successful business," one of them observed as the owner left with a huge smile.

"Hey, there's Jared!" Emily suddenly shouted as the next entrepreneur walked out. Their friend was looking for capital to grow his food truck business which was now in several cities.

Jared was asking for a $100,000 *investment*—money given to a business owner to help grow the business and create profit for everybody. In exchange, Jared was offering 15% of his business.

After he explained how the business worked, Jared provided the sharks samples of the food his trucks sold. "This is delicious!" one of them said. "But there are food trucks everywhere—the market is too crowded. I'm out."

"You need a lot of money," another shark observed, "but how am I going to make my money back? There's nothing unique about your food truck business. This offer sounds too risky."

"Like Dad always says, where there's risk, there might be a reward," Emily remarked to Ethan.

"But with all the competition that Jared has with other food trucks, the rewards are not worth the risk for the sharks," Ethan said.

And he was right—none of the sharks were willing to invest their money in Jared's company.

BETTER

ASSIST-BOT

ZIPPY

MORE
CONVENIENT

CHEAPER

"I want to be an entrepreneur like the ones on Shark Pool," Ethan said as the show ended.

"Becoming an entrepreneur isn't like choosing to work at a normal job," Mr. Tuttle chimed in. "You have to think of creative ways to improve people's lives—that's the key."

"What do you mean?" Emily asked.

"Well, opening a restaurant serves people who don't want to cook," he replied. "Creating a computer program that saves people money helps them, or inventing a machine that lets people easily exercise could be cheaper than expensive gym equipment."

"You either need to improve on something that already exists—like make a product that's cheaper or better than the alternative—or provide something that isn't already available," Mr. Tuttle added. "Then people will change how they do things and give you their business instead."

Ethan began thinking as Emily hummed a song from the musical they had seen. And then it clicked. "What if we started a theater in our town?" he said.

The wheels started turning in each of the Tuttles' minds as they realized this was an opportunity worth exploring. Besides the occasional school or church play, people in their city didn't have any opportunities to go to the theater.

It was way past the twins' bedtime when the plane landed. Ethan and Emily were so tired they could barely walk.

"Need a ride?" a familiar voice asked as the family grabbed their luggage. Nana—Mrs. Tuttle's mother—had come to drive them home.

"When we're successful entrepreneurs maybe we'll have a limousine pick us up instead," Emily commented to Ethan as she yawned.

"Got a business idea in mind, do you?" Nana asked.

"Actually, yes," Mrs. Tuttle replied. "The twins are thinking about starting a community theater. We think it might be a real business opportunity."

"That sounds intriguing," Nana replied. "I'd like to hear more. But first, let's make sure you all get a good night's rest."

The following afternoon Nana invited the family into town to talk about their business idea. "Here we are," Mr. Tuttle said as he pulled the family van to a stop.

"Wait, this is Nana's dance studio," Emily pointed out. The building looked like it hadn't been used in a while.

"Sure is," Mrs. Tuttle replied as the family walked up to the building. "I spent a lot of my youth here, learning how to dance along with half the girls in this town."

"And your mother was one of my best students... when she wasn't goofing off," Nana said, winking at her daughter. "Come on in!"

"Why did you stop doing it, Nana?" Emily asked as they stepped inside.

"The city built a recreational center a few years ago and began offering dance classes," she replied. "Because taxes fund most of their operations, they can charge much less for a dance class than I could. Many of the private dance studios, like mine, lost students and had to close."

"That seems really unfair," Ethan remarked. "I'm sorry that happened."

"Don't be sorry—that's what being an entrepreneur is all about," Nana replied. "Sometimes you win, and sometimes you lose. Plus, I wanted to retire anyway!" she added with a loud laugh.

Nana led the family through the building, swiping at some cobwebs as they walked onto the large stage.

"I want you kids to imagine this room full of people wanting to watch your plays," Nana said.

"Are you saying you'll help us?" Ethan asked eagerly. The twins jumped up and down in excitement at the thought of Nana helping them make their vision a reality. "Will you be our shark?"

"Well, I might be willing to invest in your company," Nana replied. "I want to support you in what you do, but when it comes to business, there are some important questions you have to answer. We need to figure out if you two have what it takes to be entrepreneurs."

"So, I've got five basic questions," she said. "Before I opened the dance studio many years ago, your Papa made sure I could answer each one in detail. Now it's your turn."

"Question one," she started. "*Who are you?* Not everyone likes taking risks. Many people want a safe job at a company, working a set number of hours for a set amount of money. But an entrepreneur has to work as long and hard as it takes. You sacrifice money and time for the chance at success, but you also risk failing."

"Being your own boss sounds great," Emily replied. "Plus, we've already owned a small business…"

"A *really* small business," Mrs. Tuttle whispered to her husband, thinking of the twins' little lemonade stand. She laughed softly as she unrolled some butcher paper she found. She taped the paper to the wall and began writing down the things they were talking about.

"So who are you?" Nana again asked.

"We're entrepreneurs!" the Tuttle twins quickly answered in unison.

"Second question: *what do you know?*" Nana added. "What skills or knowledge do you have to offer to customers? What makes you special to them?"

"Mom used to be in theater," Ethan answered as he twirled in the air, mimicking his mom. "She knows how to put on a good show."

"And your father has started a few successful companies before," Mrs. Tuttle added. "I think that's because he's a good problem solver, which is important."

"Dad has also taught me how to do marketing really well," Emily suggested, thinking about their food truck rally. "And Ethan has a good imagination and likes drawing!"

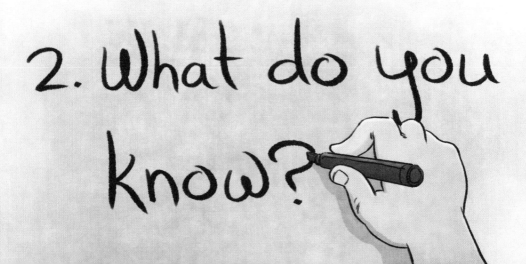

2. What do you know?

- Knowledge of the theater
- Writing

- Business Experience
- Problem Solver

- Marketing skills
- Sewing and crafts

- Math skills
- Artist
- Imagination

School Students

Food Trucks

The Tuttle Family Network

News

Cookies!

3. Who do you know?

Mrs. Tuttle started writing the third question; she already knew what Nana was going to say next. *Who do you know?*

"In almost any aspect of life, working together with people you know and trust is a key to success," Mrs. Tuttle explained. "These people are called your *network*. Who in our network has skills or knowledge that might help us with this business?"

They each started calling out names of people they knew. By the time she had finished scribbling out names, the whole sheet of butcher paper was completely filled. They had lots of friends and contacts who had skills that might help.

"Excellent!" Nana clapped in excitement. "We're off to a great start."

4. What are your resources?

"*What are your resources?*" Nana asked next. "Do you have any equipment, property, or money that you can use to start the business? How much do you have in savings?"

The twins quietly chatted together to do the math. "We only have 49 dollars, Nana," Ethan answered.

"And that's nowhere near what you'd need to put on a show," Mrs. Tuttle said. "So you really need to convince this shark here to give you some capital," she added, pointing to Nana. "Without money, this business can't even begin."

Capital

"Which leads to our fifth and final question," she replied. *"What can you contribute?* In other words, what are you offering to customers that will make their lives better?"

The twins both thought for a moment. "Dad said one way to be an entrepreneur is to provide something that isn't already available," Ethan added.

"That's right," Mrs. Tuttle said. "In our town, people go to a movie theater to watch a show. We'll have to convince them that our live performances are different, better, or less expensive. Otherwise they won't change where they go for entertainment."

"So that's what we will do... can you help us, Nana?" Emily asked.

"Well I'm certainly impressed by your passion," Nana said. "But before I invest, we have to crunch the numbers..."

5. What can you contribute?

DIFFERENT   BETTER   CHEAPER

"And that," Mr. Tuttle said, "is why you need a *business plan*—a document explaining how much the family theater will cost to operate, and also a strategy for selling enough tickets to make a profit." He ripped off a new sheet of butcher paper.

"Do we have to do this?" Emily asked.

"If you want me to give you any of my money, definitely!" Nana replied. "*You* aren't risking anything—if I let you use my building and give you my money, then I'd be the one who would lose the most if it fails. I need to see a business plan so I can see if the potential rewards are worth that risk."

"Let's start by figuring out the *budget*—a list of what everything will cost, and how much money we will need to borrow from Nana," Mr. Tuttle said.

"Good thing math is one of my skills," Ethan chuckled to himself.

"This is going to take a while," Mrs. Tuttle said, walking to the door. "I'll go get us some food."

Ethan and Emily spent half an hour coming up with a list of *expenses*—things they would have to spend money on, such as paint, building materials, new chairs, lighting, sound equipment, costumes, insurance, and more. Meanwhile, Mr. Tuttle looked up the prices of each item.

"And don't forget to add in about 2,000 dollars to purchase the rights to a play," he said.

Ethan's eyes widened as he added up all the estimated amounts. "Looks like it will be about... 23,210 dollars!" he said loudly as his mom walked in.

"Don't forget having to pay for a business license, permits, and taxes," Mrs. Tuttle added, handing everyone their food.

Ethan felt like he had been punched in the gut. "Are we going to be able to make any money?" he asked.

"Most of the cost is for new chairs. And that's more money than I have to invest," Nana explained. "Let's try to keep it under 14,000 dollars."

"But our business might be over before it even starts! It's not fair," an exasperated Ethan replied.

Emily was sad, but remembered her dad often saying how important it is to be a problem solver. "We'll just have to figure out a solution," she said.

"Right!" Mr. Tuttle said. "You're over budget, so you need to come up with creative ways to cut expenses. Any ideas?"

"I bet Ethan could write our own play," Emily suggested. "He loves making up stories and Mom could help. That will save us a lot of money."

Ethan jumped up and spoke with his mouth full of noodles. "Maybe we can find some used seats from an old movie theater or church!"

"Excellent ideas," Mr. Tuttle replied. "Let's make a few calls and see what we can find."

"I'm very impressed with your creative problem solving," Nana said enthusiastically. "These cuts should get us back on budget. You two are shaping up to be great entrepreneurs!"

"Now you need a plan to pay your expenses and make a profit," Mr. Tuttle said. "If we had 200 seats and put on six performances this year..."

"We could sell 1,200 tickets!" Ethan said. "So to pay back the 14,000 dollars, we have to sell each ticket for 12 dollars," he said, multiplying in his head.

"But that's if you paid me back in just one year," Nana said. "And then you wouldn't have a *profit margin*—extra money after paying for expenses."

"Yeah, we want lots of profit!" Emily said. "Think of all the awesome toys we can buy."

"A profit isn't just for buying toys," Mr. Tuttle said. "You'll need money to improve your business—for example, better costumes or newer chairs. If you paid it all to Nana or spent it all on toys, there would be no money left for future shows."

"Also, 12 dollars might be too high," Nana said. "How much are movie tickets these days? Your tickets might need to cost less to attract customers."

The twins decided that they would only charge $10 per ticket—giving them enough of a profit margin to pay Nana back slowly, have money to improve the business, and earn a small profit.

The twins' brains were tired. They had no idea how much there was to think about to start a business.

"Imagine what this place will look like with actors performing for sold-out audiences," Mrs. Tuttle said.

The twins pictured a family theater that was popular and helped people in the community make fun memories. Emily began leaping around the stage, excited to begin.

"But do you think people will actually come to our theater?" Ethan asked, beginning to doubt their ability to succeed.

"There's nothing else like it in town," Mr. Tuttle chimed in. "People will pay for a great experience if you give them one."

"I agree they would pay," Nana said, "which is why I want to invest. Count this shark in!"

The next few months were full of hard work. Ethan and his mom wrote a musical called "The Deep Sea Adventures of Timothy Oscar." They also conducted auditions to find the best actors who then began rehearsing regularly.

Mr. Tuttle installed benches that he got from an old church that was being renovated. He also called people in their network to see who else could help.

Mr. Miner was a talented musician and offered to write and record the music for free. Mrs. Lopez said she would make cookies for concessions, and Uncle Ben thought of a way to use projectors for the stage backgrounds to avoid having to create them.

Emily took Ethan's character designs and made costumes with Grandma Tuttle, who only spent half of the costume budget by using clothing from the secondhand store. Grandpa Tuttle got his friend, the owner of a local home improvement store, to donate supplies so he could build some signs for the front of the building along with a few stage props without going over budget.

Fixing up the building was the hardest part. The twins spent countless hours hauling out bags of trash, painting the walls, and scrubbing each surface.

Ethan and Emily were so focused on their work that they never noticed the woman who would often peer through the glass window, watching everything unfold.

Each night, when the twins were tired and wanted to relax, they instead placed posters around town and advertised online—because what would be the point of creating a theater if nobody came?

"I hope all this hard work is going to pay off," Emily sighed. "It's exhausting!"

"It will pay off—and pay us a lot of profit!" Ethan answered, imagining money raining down.

"No! Not Timothy Oscar!" one of the actors shouted, raising a trident to battle the hero.

Opening night had finally come for The Tuttle Family Theater, and Ethan and Emily nervously paced backstage as actors hurried around them, getting ready for their parts.

The audience was packed—people around town had been talking about the new community theater for weeks and were excited to see a new kind of entertainment! The props, the costumes, the music, and the projections all looked amazing!

The twins peeked through the curtain, smiling at how well the audience seemed to enjoy their play.

And then they noticed a woman sitting in the front row of the theater, watching their play with great interest and even taking notes. Neither of them knew that she had been watching them for weeks.

Who was she, they wondered?

The Tuttle family met up with Nana at the local ice cream shop after the performance. "I am so proud!" she gushed, squeezing the twins in a big hug. "The crowd loved it!"

Everybody was chatting about the play as they ate their ice cream, but all Ethan could think about was the mystery woman. "Did you guys notice a woman taking notes in the front of the audience?" he asked the others.

"I think I know who it is," Mrs. Tuttle replied. "She must be the one who put this on the cars outside, including ours," she said, showing the twins a flier for The Tarp Troupe—a theater group that was soon having its opening night on the other side of town.

"We just opened and now we already have competition?" Emily said, sounding quite frustrated. "That's not fair!"

OUR TOWN'S NEWEST THEATRICAL GROUP

THE TARP TROUPE

JOIN US FOR OUR FIRST PERFORMANCE UNDER THE TARP AT THE DOBSON FARM

Friday 7pm

Sponsored by:
The Country Market / Tarp Solutions / Atom Auto
Sanford Homes / Pump & Mill / Base Hardware

MONOPOLY
- HIGH PRICES
- POOR QUALITY
- LITTLE VARIETY

COMPETITION
- LOWEST PRICES
- BEST QUALITY
- MORE VARIETY

"You're wrong, dear," Nana quickly replied. "Competition is great! It pushes you to keep getting better and finding ways to lower your costs."

"Imagine if only one company sold ice cream," she continued, leading the twins back to the counter. "It would be a *monopoly*. They could charge whatever price they wanted, and they would have no reason to improve or offer new flavors because there would be no competition to push them to change."

"A world without tutti frutti is not one I want to live in!" Mr. Tuttle matter-of-factly said. He took his favorite ice cream flavors very seriously.

The twins stared at all the different flavors they could choose from—all because of competition.

"We can buy ice cream from many places—and the owner of this store knows it," Mrs. Tuttle added. "So he makes sure to offer a big selection of quality ice cream at an affordable price so we buy from him, rather than someone else."

"That's it!" said Ethan. "We need variety and a low price—that's how we'll succeed."

"So we do a bunch of different kinds of plays," said Emily between bites of ice cream. "But how do we lower our prices? We need to earn a profit so we can pay Nana back."

"One way is to do what your competitors are doing—getting sponsors," Mr. Tuttle responded, pointing to the flier. It listed several companies who were paying money to help support the Tarp Troupe.

The twins began whispering to one another, coming up with a plan. Ethan winked at his mom as he and Emily went to find the store manager.

Within a few minutes they returned, each grinning from ear to ear. "We have our first sponsor!" Ethan announced. The manager agreed to pay $300 to advertise his company in their program.

"The more sponsors we get, the bigger our profit is going to be!" Emily excitedly said.

The second performance started the following weekend, and though they were still working out some kinks and learning how to operate a theater, Ethan and Emily were excited to see customers filling the seats and enjoying themselves.

Looking out at the crowd, the twins then locked eyes with each other. "Look what we've built!" Ethan said to his sister. "Isn't it awesome?"

"Yeah—and our competition better watch out!" she added with a sly grin.

Emily couldn't stop smiling. She felt different—like being on Broadway, but close to home with all her family and friends supporting her.

The twins were thrilled to be their own bosses and excited to be making money. Their adventure taught them all sorts of new things each day. Now they were entrepreneurs!

Nana was waiting outside the theater as Ethan and Emily locked up later that night.

"You two have transformed this old dance studio into something amazing," she said.

"We didn't do it alone," Ethan replied. "And the fun has just begun... there's so much more to do!"

"There always is for an entrepreneur," Nana said. "Otherwise, how would sharks like me make a profit?" she smiled.

"Don't get too close!" Emily said, pushing her brother to the side. "She might bite!"

"All I want to bite right now is some ice cream," Nana said. "Let's go celebrate your hard work!"

The End

"The proper role of the entrepreneur in the market system is not typically presented in its true light, or with adequate recognition for its being the driving force for the entire market process."

—Dr. Israel M. Kirzner

Building on the work of famed economists Ludwig von Mises and F.A. Hayek, *Competition and Entrepreneurship* is acclaimed for clarifying and contextualizing the central role of the entrepreneur in the economic process—the one who is alert to discovering and acting upon new opportunities while in competition with others.

Written in 1973 but no less relevant in our day, Dr. Kirzner's classic text helps the reader understand these important economic concepts not through mathematical formulas, but verbal logic and clear explanations.

While geared towards readers with a deeper understanding of economics, this work is of interest to any parent or student seeking to better understand the economic importance of entrepreneurship.

The Author

Connor Boyack is president of Libertas Institute, a free market think tank in Utah. He is also president of The Association for Teaching Kids Economics, an organization that provides teachers with educational materials and lesson plans to teach economic ideas to their students in a fun and memorable way. Connor is the author of over a dozen books.

A California native and Brigham Young University graduate, Connor currently resides in Lehi, Utah, with his wife and two children.

The Illustrator

Elijah Stanfield is owner of Red House Motion Imaging, a media production company in Washington.

A longtime student of Austrian economics, history, and the classical liberal philosophy, Elijah has dedicated much of his time and energy to promoting the ideas of free markets and individual liberty. Some of his more notable works include producing eight videos in support of Ron Paul's 2012 presidential candidacy. He currently resides in Richland, Washington, with his wife April and their six children.

Contact us at TuttleTwins.com!

Glossary of Terms

Budget: A document listing how much money is being received and spent.

Business Plan: A document explaining how a business will operate and meet its future goals.

Entrepreneur: A business owner who identifies a need and assumes risk to meet that need in hopes of earning a profit.

Equity: The value of how much a business is worth.

Expense: The cost required to purchase something.

Investment: Providing money to a business in exchange for equity.

Monopoly: A business that does not have any competition.

Network: The people you know and interact with.

Profit Margin: The money a business has left over after paying for its expenses.

Discussion Questions

1. How would you answer each of the five questions in the book?
2. Why is there potential reward when risk is involved?
3. What are the problems with a monopoly?
4. What kind of business could you start in the next few months?
5. What prevents more people from becoming an entrepreneur?

Don't Forget the Activity Workbook!

Visit **TuttleTwins.com/BusinessWorkbook** to download the PDF and provide your children with all sorts of activities to reinforce the lessons they learned in the book!